MANNERS

by Sandra Ziegler
illustrated by Kathryn Hutton

Created by

THE CHILD'S WORLD

Distributed by CHILDRENS PRESS ®
Chicago, Illinois

CHILDRENS PRESS HARDCOVER EDITION
ISBN 0-516-06315-4

CHILDRENS PRESS PAPERBACK EDITION
ISBN 0-516-46315-2

Library of Congress Cataloging-in-Publication Data

Ziegler, Sandra, 1938-
   Manners / by Sandra Ziegler ; illustrated by Kathryn Hutton.
      p. cm. — (What are they?)
   Summary: Presents situations in which children react in ways
that show they have good manners.
   ISBN 0-89565-377-X
   1. Etiquette for children and youth.   [1. Etiquette.]
I. Hutton, Kathryn, ill.   II. Title.   III. Series.
BJ1857.C5Z54   1988
395'.122—dc 19   88-15013
                                     CIP
                                      AC

1 2 3 4 5 6 7 8 9 10 11 12 R 99 98 97 96 95 94 93 92 91 90 89

MANNERS

Two "ladies" walk along my street.
They smile at everyone they meet.
They say, "Good morning. How are you?"
And what do you think the people do?
"Fine, thank you," they nod and say.
"Isn't this a perfect day?"
The reason that I know all this—
The "ladies" are me and my friend, Chris.

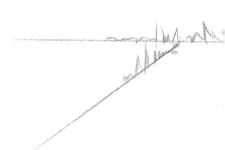

What are good manners?

Asking your friend to come inside,
instead of letting her stand in the
rain, is good manners.

And so is saying, "Let me hang up
your raincoat."

If your friend takes off her boots,
instead of tracking muddy prints all
the way to your room, she's using
good manners.

And letting your friend help you
choose what to play, instead of
deciding for her, is good manners.

When you get an invitation to a birth-
day party, and you call to say you're
coming, that's showing good manners.

And so is writing a thank-you note
when your friend brings a gift to *your*
party.

When you are serving tea to a
friend, and another friend arrives,
showing good manners is saying,
"Come in."

And it's showing good manners to
pass around the cookies for everyone
to share.

Showing good manners is splitting the last of the lemonade with your friend when you are both hot and thirsty from running a race.

Using your napkin to wipe messy
fingers shows good manners.

So does chewing with your mouth
closed and not talking with your
mouth full.

When you and your friend paint
pictures at her house . . .

you show good manners when you
help wash the brushes and put the
paints away.

Showing good manners is answering
the telephone politely . . .

and telling your mom that the store
called to say her order is in.

When you spend the night with a
friend, showing good manners is . . .

saying ''hello'' to your friend's
parents when you arrive, . . .

and it's saying ''good-bye'' and ''thank-you'' when you leave.

When you hold the door for your teacher, that's showing good manners.

So is waiting your turn and not push-
ing at the water fountain when you
come in from recess.

When Mom and Dad are in their room, and you knock on the door instead of walking right in, that's showing good manners.

When you show good manners,
people know you care about them
and not just about yourself.

Have you used good manners today?